Operating the Spirit of Prayer

Operating the Spirit of Prayer

A Deep and Concise Exposition on the Subject of Prayer

Anthony Adefarakan

GLOEM, CANADA

CONTENTS

Dedication	1
Acknowledgement	2
Introduction	4
1. Prayer Defined	6
2. Types of Prayer	8
3. Who Can Pray?	13
4. How to Approach God in Prayer	15
5. What Can We Pray About?	24

CONTENTS

6 | How Often Should We Pray? **26**

7 | God's Attitude to Our Prayers **28**

8 | Hindrances to Answered Prayers **33**

9 | The Ministry of Our Helper in Prayer **39**

| Conclusion **45**

| WHY YOU REALLY NEED JESUS! **47**

| PRAYER POINTS **52**

| BECOME A FINANCIAL PARTNER WITH JESUS **54**

| About the Author **57**

CONTENTS

| 60

| 61

Dedication

I dedicate this book to God Almighty for His goodness and faithfulness in making His Word available to me. All glory to His Holy Name.

Also to everyone desirous of a vibrant prayer life, accessing the throne of grace for answers to prayers on a daily basis, I am in agreement with you all and I decree that grace for an effective prayer life is coming upon you in Jesus' Name.

Acknowledgement

I sincerely acknowledge my Eternal Father, Who alone is the Source of all wisdom. He is the Author and Finisher of my faith and it is of His fullness that the contents of this book have been drawn.

Also, I want to profoundly appreciate my dear parents – Prince and Mrs. Timothy Adefarakan – for bringing me up in the way of the Lord and for instilling righteousness consciousness in me. The wonderful education foundation I was given, coupled with their constant encouragement has empowered me to reach heights that were once beyond my imagination.

My most special appreciation goes to my sweetheart, Abisolami; without her help and support I would never have enjoyed the conducive atmosphere needed to publish this book. I appreciate your love, encouragement, and the support you give at all times. Thank you so much. I love you my Baby!

And to all my mentors in Ministry, I appreciate you all. Your investments in my life are not in vain. May the Lord reward you all in Jesus' Name.

Introduction

There is this popular song we used to sing in Church those days when we were younger. It goes thus:

Prayer is the Key, Prayer is the Key,
Prayer is the Master Key,
Jesus started with Prayer,
and ended with Prayer,
Prayer is the Master Key.

I'm sure someone reading this still remembers that song.

Now, for prayer to really be a Master key, it means it has the ability to open several doors. And that's exactly what prayer does. It opens various doors and also shuts various doors depending on the direction the user turns it.

Furthermore, there is no way humanity can relate with divinity without prayers, because that's the only means of communication we have if we ever want to be in touch with our Father in Heaven.

The contents of this book are all Bible-based teachings on the subject of prayer and will deliver results every time they are applied because the Word of God is forever settled in Heaven (Psalm 119:89).

I pray as you read on, God's grace to begin operating the spirit of prayer will rest upon you in Jesus' Name.

Anthony Adefarakan.

1

Prayer Defined

Several definitions abound when it comes to the subject of prayer because different religions and dictionaries have described prayer to mean several things; but for the purpose of this book, we will be defining prayer as simply talking to God. That's simple enough to understand. To pray is to communicate with God.

Now, talking to God could be about anything at all. It could be to ask for help, to appreciate Him, to make certain requests, to get certain clarifications or just simply to adore Him.

One other important thing to take note of as far as prayer is concerned is that it takes into account that God hears and listens to the prayers of His people. Psalm 65:2 ASV says: *"O thou that hearest prayer, Unto thee shall all flesh come."*

If God doesn't hear or answer when we pray, then it would be wrong to say prayer is talking to God. But because He hears and answers, we have confidence when we offer our prayers to Him.

1 John 5:14-15 KJV affirms this:
"And this is the confidence that we have in him, that, if we ask any thing according to his will, he heareth us: And if we know that he hear us, whatsoever we ask, we know that we have the petitions that we desired of him."

2

Types of Prayer

Ephesians 6:18 NIV says: *"pray...on all occasions with all kinds of prayer..."*

The *"all kinds of prayer"* stated in the text above suggests that different kinds of prayer exist. That is, prayer has different elements or types.

In this chapter, we will be considering six (6) types of prayer with their various applications in the Christian faith.

1. **Worship and Praises:** this involves showing a deep reverence for God and giving Him glory for Who He is and for what He does. It's an expression of admiration,

honour and respect for God which can be accompanied by singing beautiful melodies to Him as well as talking to Him about how wonderful He is.

In Psalm 8:1 KJV, David said *"O LORD, our Lord, how excellent is thy name in all the earth! Who has set thy glory above the heavens."* That's an expression of worship. David was talking to God about His own greatness; that's a form of prayer. And as a matter of fact, worship is the highest form of prayer. God highly treasures those who offer Him worship and praises.

2. **Thanksgiving:** this is a prayer of gratitude. It takes into account all the good things God has done. We engage in this form of prayer when we remember His goodness and mercy as well as all the benefits we have received from Him. 1 Thessalonians 5:18 says it is God's will for us to engage in this type of prayer. He loves to receive our thanks. So, when we pray

in this way, we are talking to God about what we are grateful for.

3. **Supplication:** this is the most popular from of prayer because it has to do with making requests. Matthew 7:7 NIV says *"Ask and it will be given to you; seek and you will find; knock and the door will be opened to you."*

   When we make supplications, we are asking God for something. It could be for His help, intervention, assistance, or simply His provision. Individuals can make supplications, groups of people can make supplications and even nations can do same. It's all about directing certain requests to God for His attention.

4. **Petition:** this is also a form of supplication, but it's different in that it holds God accountable for His Words. We can petition God in prayer based on His promises; we can ask Him to fulfill what He has promised in His Word based on the fact

OPERATING THE SPIRIT OF PRAYER

that He is not a man that should lie (Numbers 23:18).

5. **Intercession:** this is the type of prayer that has to do with standing in the gap for others. It is a highly rewarding form of prayer because it is practically selfless and as a result sacrificial. Here, you talk to God on behalf of others. You present other people's needs and problems to God for His intervention. God highly cherishes and honors intercessors.

6. **Praying in the Holy Ghost:** this has to do with talking to God in a spiritual language (that you never learned). It's a language (utterance) given to you by the Holy Ghost for spiritual communication. It's a form of coded language. We will talk more about this later on in this book.

Now, it is very important to note that all these elements of prayer can be present every time you pray. You don't have to substitute or separate any. That is, each time you pray, worship, supplication, thanksgiving and other forms of prayer may be present (all at once). You don't have to do supplication on Mondays, intercession on Tuesdays, or Thanksgiving on Fridays; you can do all every time you pray. They are all interwoven elements.

3

Who Can Pray?

Jesus taught His disciples to pray in Matthew 6:9-13 KJV (popularly called The Lord's Prayer). Let's take a look at it:

"After this manner therefore pray ye: Our Father which art in heaven, Hallowed be thy name.

Thy kingdom come. Thy will be done in earth, as it is in heaven.

Give us this day our daily bread.

And forgive us our debts, as we forgive our debtors.

And lead us not into temptation, but deliver us from evil: For thine is the kingdom, and the power, and the glory, for ever. Amen."

Notice how Jesus started the prayer; He said

'Our Father which art in heaven.' That means you must be a child (either son or daughter) of God to be able to relate with Him in prayer. God is the Creator of all things and everyone, but He is not a Father to everyone. John 1:12 says you must be born again to be able to call God your Father.

One other important thing to note is that your prayer must be offered to God in the Name of Jesus (John 14:13-14). You don't pray to anyone else or to any god/deity; only to the Almighty God – Daniel 6:7, 10 and 11.

That being said, if you are not yet a child of God, the only prayer He expects to hear from you is a prayer of mercy (repentance from your sins and asking Him to forgive and save you by His grace).

So are you a child of God? If yes, He is eagerly expecting to hear your unique voice in prayer.

4

How to Approach God in Prayer

Certain approaches have been identified as far as talking to God in prayer is concerned. These approaches are as revealed in the very Word of God and as such are worth following.

They are:

1. Psalm 100:2 KJV – *'...come before His Presence with singing.'*
   Regardless of your situation at the moment, God wants you to come before Him with singing. The Bible says in verse 4 of this same Psalm 100 that you should enter His courts with praise. You don't

want to approach the throne of grace with lamentations and complaints. That's not the right way for sons and daughters to approach their Heavenly Father.

You get His attention faster when you approach Him with praises because Psalm 22: 3 says He inhabits the praises of His people.

2. Psalm 95:2 KJV– *'Let us come before His Presence with thanksgiving...'*

   This is another important way God wants to be approached. It calls into account the past benefits you have enjoyed from Him. He expects you to show some gratitude for Who He is and all He has done when you come before Him in prayer. Psalm 100:4 says you are to enter His gates with thanksgiving. That's how to secure His attention in prayer.

3. Hebrews 4:16 KJV – *'Let us therefore come boldly unto the throne of grace...'*

   God sees us as children, not slaves, and He expects us to approach Him with the

OPERATING THE SPIRIT OF PRAYER

same mindset. He wants us to approach Him boldly, recognizing Him as our good and loving Father.

Romans 8:15 NIV says *"The Spirit you received does not make you slaves, so that you live in fear again; rather, the Spirit you received brought about your adoption to sonship. And by him we cry, "Abba, Father."*

Don't approach God as if you are not sure if He's going to welcome you or not. Come before His throne with boldness and assurance of your relationship with Him.

4. Hebrews 11:6 BSB – *'...anyone who approaches Him must believe that He exists and that He rewards those who earnestly seek Him.'*

When approaching God in prayer, you have to come by faith. You must come to God believing that He's there and that He will answer you. Mark 11:24 says whatever you desire when you pray, believe that you have received it and it shall be yours. You can't relate with an unseen God except by faith. You need faith to access the throne of grace.

5. Matthew 7:7-10 KJV - *'Ask, and it shall be given you...or what man is there of you, whom if his son ask bread, will he give him a stone? Or if he ask a fish, will he give him a serpent?'*

   When it comes to prayers, you have to be as specific as possible. If you need fish, ask God for fish and if it is bread, ask Him for bread. Don't be vague or ambiguous in your prayers. God knows your heart as well as what you need before you pray but He still wants you to mention it to Him when praying. Look at the story of Blind Bartimaeus in Mark 10:46-52, Jesus knew quite alright that he was blind (as everyone could notice) but He still asked him what he wanted; it was when the man said he wanted his sight that Jesus gave him his sight. If you need a baby from God for instance, specify the kind and the gender of your interest to Him. Also, don't just ask God for a job, tell Him the exact kind of job you want. Learn to be specific when talking to God in prayer.

6. Matthew 6: 6-8 KJV – *'...when thou prayest, enter into thy closet, and ...pray to thy Father which is in secret...'* Jesus taught His disciples to pray secretly without drawing attention to themselves. He said they should go into their closets and talk to their Father in secret with the assurance that their Father Who sees what is done in the secret would reward them openly. He was actually teaching them to not engage in prayer as a show business. He also warned them against using vain repetitions when praying because God doesn't answer prayers based on much speaking or the number of times such prayer is offered. And what He said to His disciples then He is also saying to us now as His followers. Pray in the secret and avoid vain repetitions.

7. Ephesians 6:18 KJV – *'Praying always with all prayer and supplication in the Spirit...'*

    To pray in the Spirit is to allow your spirit pray instead of your mind. The Holy Spirit has His peculiar language of communication which is popularly known as 'tongues'. He bestows this peculiar ability to communicate in His language when He comes upon you. The most effective way to relate with God, Who is a Spirit, is to pray in the Spirit (in the language of the Holy Ghost). John 4:23-24 says God is a Spirit and He seeks those who will worship Him in spirit and in truth. We will talk more about praying in the spirit later on in this book.

8. Matthew 6:9-13, 33 KJV – *'After this manner therefore pray ye...Thy Kingdom come...'*

    Be kingdom-minded and let it reflect in your prayers. God's most special interest is all about establishing His kingdom among men. That's why He sent Jesus down to die in the first place. It is a very smart way to pray when you begin to talk to God about His area of special interest – 'Thy kingdom come'. Amos 3:3 says for two people to walk together, there must be agreement. God loves to redeem souls from the power of sin, that should be what you love too and it should be what you talk Him about often. Verse 33 of Matthew 6 says you should seek first God's kingdom and His righteousness with the promise that every other thing would be added to you (whether you pray about them or not).

9. 1 Samuel 2:3 KJV – *'...the LORD is a God of knowledge, and by Him actions are weighed.'* God knows all things, including the contents of every heart. So, when we come to Him in prayer, our hearts must be free from all manners of offences, grudges, malice, bitterness, hatred, envy, resentments etc. God highly

treasures those with pure hearts. So, cleanse your heart prior to approaching Him in prayer. Also, because the Lord is a God of knowledge, the posture you take in prayer doesn't really matter to Him as long as your heart is right before Him. If you like, you may kneel down, prostrate, bend down, put your head in-between your knees, raise your hands, stand, sit, lie down, squat, walk around or take any posture you want. None of these postures guarantee answers to prayer. You may feel comfortable with one posture or you may feel 'spiritual' with another; it all depends on you and the situation you find yourself in. For instance, you can't be kneeling down to pray while you are driving, it is not possible. And just because someone kneels down to pray doesn't mean God will answer their prayers more than the person who sits down to pray. All God is looking for is your sincere heart and pure motive when you pray. He answers you based on what He finds in your heart. 1 Samuel 16:7 says God looks at the heart (not outward appearances).

5

What Can We Pray About?

John 14:13-14 KJV says: *"And whatsoever ye shall ask in my name, that will I do, that the Father may be glorified in the Son. If ye shall ask any thing in my name, I will do it."*

Also, Philippians 4:6 NLT says: *"Don't worry about anything; instead, pray about everything. Tell God what you need, and thank him for all he has done."*

From these two scriptures, it is apparent that we can pray about anything and everything.

As far as God is concerned, nothing is too small

OPERATING THE SPIRIT OF PRAYER

or too big to discuss with Him. You can talk to Him about your worries, fears, concerns, results, projects, marriage, family, career, journey, plans, boss, children, finances, health, internet connection, business ideas, memory, sleep patterns, troublesome child, uncooperative spouse etc.

Why is this necessary? It's because God knows all things and can do all things. So there is nothing you cannot discuss with the Creator of Heaven and Earth. He knows everything about everything.

6

How Often Should We Pray?

In Luke 18:1 KJV, Jesus said *"...men ought always to pray, and not to faint"* and 1 Thessalonians 5:17 also says *"Pray without ceasing"*.

From these two scriptures, the Lord expects us to pray all the time (without fainting or giving up). So by implication, you are to pray when you are fine and when you are not fine; when it's convenient and when it's not; when things are working and when they are not working; when things are going your way and when they are going against you; when you are tired and when you are strong; when you have abundance and when you are in want etc.

You are to keep praying as long as you are breathing. As a matter of fact, prayer is to your spirit-man what oxygen is to your physical body. You are to keep breathing prayer every time and everywhere. And that's the advantage of praying in the Spirit as it makes you more conscious of the spiritual environment than your physical surroundings. We will talk more about this later.

There is no time you shouldn't be praying. If you prayed to receive a miracle, you also need to pray so as to not lose it. And if peradventure you lose it, you will need to pray in order to recover it.

You will never get to a spiritual level where prayer will no longer be needed. In fact, the higher you go, the more you pray.

7

God's Attitude to Our Prayers

In the previous sections of this book we have been able to establish that God does exist and that He answers prayers. Now we will be considering His attitude to us when we pray as well as His responses to our prayers:

1. **God delights in our prayers.** He takes pleasure in listening to the prayers offered by His children according to Proverbs 15:8 and 29. So, you are not bothering Him when you pray; He's actually enjoying your prayers and of course, He responds.

2. **God hears and answers.** 1 John 5:14-15 says the confidence we have in Him is that He hears us when we pray. And Psalm 65:2 as well as Jeremiah 33:3 point to the fact that God hears and answers prayers offered to Him.

   However, it is worthy of note that His answers may not always be what you expect; He usually answers in your best interest. For example, in 1 Kings 19:4-8 Elijah asked the Lord to take his life but instead of killing him as he requested, God fed him and strengthened him.

   Also, in Jonah 4:3-11 Jonah prayed to die but God kept him alive. That's why before you pray, it is wise to have an understanding of His will and purpose; then channel your prayers in that line –like praying His Word back to Him.

3. **God reveals.** Deuteronomy 29:29 says the secret things belong to God but the ones that are revealed belong to us. The things that are hidden to you are very

open before Him. There is nothing hidden before the Lord; and if you want, He can share some of them with you when you ask Him in prayer like Daniel 2: 17-22 declares.

He says in Jeremiah 33:3 KJV, *"Call unto me; and I will answer thee, and shew thee great and mighty things, which thou knowest not."*

What God shows you in prayer, you can't get in any higher institution of learning or seminaries. Call on God for insights today; He still reveals.

4. **God forgives.** According to Mark 11:25-26, we obtain forgiveness when we pray (provided we forgive our own offenders though). When this happens, the heavens remain open over our prayers.

5. **God directs.** In Psalm 32:8 God promises to instruct us, teach us and guide us. Also in Isaiah 30:21 He promises to direct us on the path we are to walk. We receive divine direction when we pray and as a

result we avoid unnecessary mistakes and poor choices.

6. **God gives what we ask for.** Matthew 7:7 says *"Ask, and it shall be given you..."* and John 14:14 says *"If ye shall ask any thing in my name, I will do it."* When we ask God for bread, we don't get stone. We receive what we ask for in prayer because God is faithful and dependable.

7. **God gives more than we ask for.** Ephesians 3:20 says God is able to do exceedingly abundantly above whatever we can ask or imagine according to His power that works in us. God is so generous that He doesn't just give us what we ask for; He usually gives more. Psalm 23:5 says God anointed me with oil, my cup runs over (overflows). God gives His blessings in loads (Psalm 68:19).

These among others are the responses we can expect whenever we talk to God in prayer. He's so faithful, and thus can be trusted to do what He says He would do.

ANTHONY ADEFARAKAN

8

Hindrances to Answered Prayers

By hindrances to answered prayers we mean factors that can prevent prayers from being answered. Several of such factors exist, but we will only be considering four (4) in this book.

They are:

1. **Sin** – this is one factor that will make prayers go unanswered any day. It simply cuts off your communication channel with heaven.

    John 9:31 says God doesn't hear sinners; and in Isaiah 59:1-2, it is written that the hand of the Lord is not shortened that it cannot save neither is his ear heavy that it cannot hear, but sin has hidden His face from you so that He will not hear. Sin is a major hindrance to answered prayers. Habakkuk 1:13 says God cannot look on iniquity; so how is He going to hear prayers offered in sin? You can't be in sin and still be in fellowship with God; that's one factor that causes prayers to be offered in vain without results. Sin of any degree (light or heavy as people call it) will cut off your connection. You will just be shouting, but He won't hear you. You must solve the problem of sin through the Cleansing Blood of Jesus Christ before you can begin to pray with expectation of answers. He has said it before in His Word and He is saying it again: BE YE HOLY FOR I AM HOLY!

2. **Not Forgiving Others** – although this is also a sin, it's a special category as God really pays great attention to it. Withholding forgiveness from your offenders can

deny you God's forgiveness which will in turn rain down God's judgment upon you. Until you forgive others, God has no business forgiving you. Mark 11: 25-26 says when you stand praying, forgive, if you have ought against any so that your Father also may forgive you. But if you don't, your Father will not forgive your trespasses too. And if He refuses to forgive you, your prayers will not be heard let alone being answered.

Release your offenders including your spouses and children (if they are); you need God's forgiveness to secure answers to your prayers.

3. **Maltreating Your Wife** – this applies to husbands. 1 Peter 3:7 says the way you treat your wife can determine if your prayers will be answered or hindered. It reads: *"Likewise, ye husbands, dwell with them according to knowledge, giving honour unto the wife, as unto the weaker vessel, and as being heirs together of the grace*

of life; that your prayers be not hindered." (KJV).

So if you refuse to treat your wife with some honour and respect, the heavens may be closed to your prayers and that's not a position you want to find yourself in.

Smart husbands know that treating their wives well facilitates answers to their prayers, so they don't cheat on their wives, beat them or make them sad. Your marriage is a spiritual transaction; and it's high time you started treating it as such.

4. **Forces of Darkness** – In Daniel 10: 10-14, the answers to the prayer of Daniel was delayed for 21 days by a major prince of darkness. Thank God for divine intervention, he would have been totally denied those answers. Get this straight! The devil's main assignment is to oppose God's plans and purposes concerning your life. So you will have to deal with him decisively. Put on God's whole

armour according to Ephesians 6: 10-18 and engage in some binding and casting dimension of prayer to command a release of your delayed answers. Like Daniel, never stop praying; remain tenacious and make sure the devil doesn't cheat you out of what rightfully belongs to you.

In your health for example, pray if you need healing and command all forces working against your healing to give up in the Name of Jesus – 2 Corinthians 10: 3-6.

Possess a militant attitude when dealing with these forces; they will always bow to those who recognize and use their authority in Christ Jesus – Luke 10:17-19.

It is however worthy of note that you have to submit yourself to God first before you can expect the devil and his cohorts to honour your commands – James 4:7. That's very important.

You don't want to experience the kind of embarrassment the sons of Sceva faced when they tried to cast out some demons using the Name of Jesus they hadn't submitted to – Acts 19:13-17. The devil knows those who belong to Jesus and those who do not. Don't attempt to deal with any agent of the devil until you have fully surrendered your life to Jesus Christ. It's His Name that gets the job done, not your grammatical construction or eloquence.

Having considered these four hindrances to answered prayers, we should never become their victims again. Run away from sin and deal with forces of darkness opposing God's will in your life and your prayers will never go unanswered again.

9

The Ministry of Our Helper in Prayer

God is a Spirit and He has deep-seated counsels and purposes concerning all His creation – including us His children.

Isaiah 55:8-9 says the way He thinks differs completely from the way we think – so, to access His great will and align our prayers with it, we need the ministry of the Helper – the Holy Spirit.

Now, Who is this Holy Spirit? Let's get to meet Him:

1. The Holy Spirit is the third Person in the

Trinity. He's next after God the Father and God the Son.

2. He oversees all the affairs of God's Kingdom here on earth. He came at Pentecost – Acts 2:1-11 (in the upper room) and He has been around since then.
3. According to 1 Corinthians 2:12, He helps us to know the things that God has freely given to us so we can claim and possess them.
4. According to John 14:26, He teaches us all things – including things to pray about, and reminds us what we have been taught by Jesus.
5. According to John 16:13, He guides us into all truth and He shows us things to come. He literally grants us access into the future. He reveals divine plans to us and helps us to walk in them.
6. He intercedes for us. He prays on our behalf and also through us in perfect alignment with God's will; so we can never

miss it when He helps us in prayers – Romans 8:26-27.

It's however important to note that even though He is always present with God's children, we still need to consciously engage His services if we must benefit from His help – like switching on the Power Generator in order to see lights come on. And one way we achieve that is by praying in His language – speaking in tongues or simply praying in the Holy Ghost –Jude 20.

Concerning this speaking in unknown tongues, 1 Corinthians 14:2,14 says when you pray in the Spirit or sing in the Spirit, only God understands what the Spirit is saying through you. Even you may not know what you are praying about – but God knows you are praying in line with His will and He answers without delay.

No devil can hinder any prayer offered in tongues because He knows nothing about it. It's such a wonderful asset to be able to pray in the Holy Ghost.

How then can we begin to take advantage of this great privilege? Accept the Lordship of Jesus Christ over your life, ask Him for the baptism of the Holy Spirit (John 1:29-34) and start engaging the ministry of the Helper. It's such a great way to pray.

I will close this chapter with the story of a certain missionary who was serving in one remote community. He couldn't speak the peoples' local language so he got himself a translator.

One day, he was in his house when suddenly he began to hear some disturbing and rather violent sounds of drums accompanied with some chants close by. He asked his translator what that meant and he told him it meant they were going to die. Apparently that's what the villagers did customarily whenever they were going to carry out some executions.

Upon realizing it was the end, this missionary said his last prayers and came out to meet the vio-

OPERATING THE SPIRIT OF PRAYER

lent villagers. But the moment they saw him, something unusual happened. Instead of attacking him as planned, they started bowing down to him, chanting something else in their language. The man became surprised and asked his translator what that meant; he told him the villagers were saying he's a god. That is, upon seeing this missionary, they saw something about him that made them conclude he's a god and that's why they were paying obeisance to him.

That's how this missionary escaped death and carried out his assignment in that community.

Now, when this man returned to his home church months after and shared the testimony of how God mysteriously delivered him, a brother in the church became so curious and asked what day and time that happened. Upon telling him, the brother was so surprised. He told the missionary 'that was the exact day the Holy Spirit prompted me to pray for you'. He didn't know what to pray about so he prayed in the Holy Ghost. He allowed the Holy Spirit to pray through him by praying in tongues – in the language of the Holy Spirit. And the Lord Who knows the mind of the Spirit understood what needed to be done and used the prayer of the brother in the city to deliver a missionary who was about to be executed in a far-away village.

That's how potent praying in the Holy Ghost can be.

Your Helper is someone who makes your task easier for you; so to not engage His services is to consciously subscribe to struggle.

Connect with the Holy Ghost today and let Him start praying through you. If you need help in getting this experience, you can talk to your local Pastor; he will be able to guide you further. It's not an experience any believer should be without. Your Helper is always willing to help you provided you engage his services.

Conclusion

In the course of this book, the Lord has revealed great biblical truths to us about the subject of prayer. The purpose is not just to know, document or preach them, rather they were revealed so that we can walk in them; so that we can begin to operate the spirit of prayer.

According to John 8:32, only the truth that is known sets free. So, go over these concepts one by one and determine to build up your prayer life for Kingdom impact here on earth. To be prayerless is to be powerless; and your life will never be greater than your prayer life permits.

Jesus said in John 13:17(NLT) - *"You know these things- now do them! That is the path of blessing."*

As you determine to begin to operate this Spirit

of Prayer, may the Lord shine His light into every department of your life and give you your much awaited testimonies in Jesus' Name.

WHY YOU REALLY NEED JESUS!

You might have heard a lot of Preachers talk about the importance of surrendering one's life to Jesus and even the dangers of not doing so at one time or the other without you being really moved. But with these three (3) important reasons highlighted below, I strongly believe you will not need another sermon before deciding to yield to His saving grace regardless of your religious beliefs.

1. **You have an Enemy to overcome:** There is an adversary who is all out to steal from you, kill you and destroy you regardless of your level of education, moral uprightness, societal influence or even religious beliefs. He is Devil by name (John 10:10, 1 Peter 5: 8), and he doesn't release any of

his captives until he completely destroys their souls in hell. The ONLY One Who can deliver you from his manipulations and also save your soul from him is Jesus Christ.

2. **You have an Appointment to keep:** Being alive and reading this implies you have a very important and inevitable appointment to keep. It is an appointment with death (Hebrews 9:27). Death is the sure end of all mortals (of which you are part); and to enable you prepare for this appointment without fear of eternal damnation, you need Jesus. He is the ONLY One Who has power over death (Revelation 1:18).

3. **You have a Judge to face:** Upon departure from this earth, you will have to stand before a judgment throne to render an account of your earthly life (Hebrews 9:27, Romans 14:12). The outcome of this judgment is what will determine your eternal abode which will either be Heaven

or the Lake of fire. Interestingly, the Judge Who will preside over your case and also decide where you will spend your eternity is Jesus (John 5:21-30, 2 Timothy 4:1). I perceive you are thinking "is God not our Judge? Why Jesus?' Well, you are not wrong. But God the Father Himself is the One Who handed over all the judgment to His Son, Jesus Christ. Read the verse 22 of that John chapter 5. So Jesus is the ONLY One Who has the power to either judge you guilty or guiltless in eternity.

Now that you know these, the wisest thing you can do for yourself is to quickly establish a relationship with Jesus, since you don't even know how close your appointment with death is. To do this, say this prayer aloud:

"Lord Jesus, I am a sinner and I cannot help myself. Wash me in your precious blood and make me a new creature. I open the door of my heart to you today, come into my life and become my Lord and Savior. Grant me the grace to overcome the devil, prepare me for eternity

and help me to escape the judgment reserved for sinners. Thank You Jesus for saving me. Amen."

Congratulations! You are now SAVED. Go and sin no more.

To learn more about your new relationship with Jesus, kindly send an Email to info@gloem.org or emancipation4souls@yahoo.com, we will send you a material that will help you. You can also call, text or send whatsapp message to +1 587 9735910 or +1 587 9695910 for further assistance.

And to learn more about God, His Word and His plans for your life, kindly visit our Facebook page [*https://www.facebook.com/gloem.org*] for daily meditation in the Word of God (all year round) and our Blog page [*https://gloem.org/my-blog*] for life transforming publications.

You are also invited to listen to Freedom Podcast: The Official Weekly Podcast of Global Emancipation Ministries – Calgary via https://anchor.fm/gloem

All these great resources capable of developing your spiritual stamina will help you become an overcomer in life regardless of what comes your way.

PRAYER POINTS

1. Father, thank You for opening my eyes to the truths contained in this book.
2. Father, please cause every one of my prayers to be answered speedily.
3. I cancel everything hindering answers to my prayers in Jesus' Name.
4. God of all possibilities, please cause my grass to become green again.
5. From today, my breakthrough shall no longer be delayed in Jesus' Name.
6. Father, beginning from now, please release upon me and my household the ability to pray effectively with results by the help of your Holy Spirit in the Name of Jesus.
7. Father, I thank You for answering all my

prayers. Glory be to Your Holy Name. Hallelujah!

BECOME A FINANCIAL PARTNER WITH JESUS

At *Global Emancipation Ministries - Calgary*, our mandate is *to liberate men through the knowledge of the Truth* and our mission statement is *creating channels through which men can encounter the Truth - [Isaiah 61:1-3; John 8:32, 36; I Thessalonians 5:24]*.

Our Ministerial Activities include Rural and Urban Evangelical Outreaches, Prison Evangelism, Hospital Ministrations, Mobilization for Missions Support, Teaching of the undiluted Word of God, Scripture-Based Seminars, Discipleship, Training of Field Missionaries and Empowerment of underprivileged ones among other Field Ministerial Tasks.

If you sense the Lord is calling you to reach out to the lost by engaging in any of these activities or by assisting those involved with your resources, please feel free to join us. Let us come together as we take the Gospel of our Lord Jesus Christ to the hurting and forgotten ones. [Mark 16:15-20].

Please join us in these kingdom projects by making your weekly, monthly, quarterly or annual donations to Global Emancipation Ministries – Calgary.

You can visit the "GIVE" section on our website, www.gloem.org, to learn about the ways to give.

For acknowledgement, please advise your donations to us by email: info@gloem.org or emancipation4souls@yahoo.com, and kindly include your details i.e. name, address, email and location. Alternatively, you can simply call +1 587 9735910 to do same.

You can also volunteer your gifts and talents in the service of the Lord through our ministerial platforms regardless of your location. To get information on how to go about this, please visit www.gloem.org and contact us via email: info@gloem.org or emancipation4souls@yahoo.com.

God bless you.

About the Author

By the special grace of God, **Anthony O. Adefarakan** is the privileged President of **Global Emancipation Ministries - Calgary (GLOEM)** with headquarters in Canada, North America and **Emancipating Truth Ministry International (ETMI)** with headquarters in Nigeria, West Africa.

The Lord called him into the field ministry in February 2008 with the mandate to liberate men through the knowledge of the Truth, and by December 2012 he was ordained and commissioned as the Pioneer Pastor – in – Charge of The Redeemed Christian Church of God, Revelation Parish, Shalom Area under Delta Province III, Nigeria where he served until 1st February 2015 when he officially handed over to a new Pastor in order to focus on his field ministry to which the Lord had earlier called him and for which the authority of the church had already prayed and released him to undertake.

On 29th September 2013, he was awarded a Post Graduate Diploma in Tent – Making Mission from the Redeemed Christian School of Missions, Nigeria (RECSOM, Asaba Campus) where he also had the privilege to train Pastors and Missionaries as a lecturer in 2017.

Since the commissioning of his field ministry in 2015 he has had the opportunity to lead his ministry officers to field ministrations in different Prisons, Hospitals, Orphanages, Rural communities, Camp settlements, Markets, Local churches among other places with great successes on all occasions – such as salvation of sinners, healing of the sick, financial empowerment of mission churches, provision of relief materials to the poor, provision of medical services to the underprivileged, baptism in the Holy Ghost, deliverance from demonic oppression, release of inmates just to mention a few - all to the glory of God Who alone is the Doer.

He is the author of other best-selling titles such as *The Law of Kinds, Learning From the Ants, The Immutability of God's Counsel, Surely there is an End, Life Applicable lessons from the Book of Ruth, One thing is Needful Weekly Devotional Guide, Life Applicable Revelations from God's Word* (Volumes 1 and 2) among others.

He is blissfully married to Ifeoluwa A. Adefarakan and their marriage is fruitful to the glory of God.

Jesus is his Message, Freedom is the Outcome!

Isaiah 61:1-3

www.ingramcontent.com/pod-product-compliance
Lightning Source LLC
Chambersburg PA
CBHW021431070526
44577CB00001B/162